# Let's Do Yoga

## Coloring and Activity Book

Kerry Alison Wekelo

Illustrations by Irene Olds on the front cover

© 2012 Kerry Alison Wekelo. All rights reserved.

No part of this book may be reproduced, stored in a retrieval system, or transmitted by any means without the written permission of the author.

Published by Peaceful Daily

ISBN: 978-0-9970143-8-9 (paperback)
       978-0-9982579-3-8 (ebook)

Any people depicted in stock imagery provided by Thinkstock are models, and such images are being used for illustrative purposes only.

Certain stock imagery © Thinkstock.

Prepress by Perseus-Design.com

This book is printed on acid-free paper.

Because of the dynamic nature of the Internet, any web addresses or links contained in this book may have changed since publication and may no longer be valid. The views expressed in this work are solely those of the author and do not necessarily reflect the views of the publisher, and the publisher hereby disclaims any responsibility for them.

This coloring and activity book is a compliment to the Audrey's Journey series. Each page provides a mindful activity or yoga pose. This book is the perfect resource for teachers, parents, camp counselors, yoga instructors or anyone that works or plays with kids.

# Yoga

The term yoga comes from a Sanskrit word meaning "union." Yoga combines feeling your body through exercise and breathing.

# Poses

The poses in yoga help you feel your body and make you strong.

Stretching makes your muscles more flexible
so you can move in all directions.

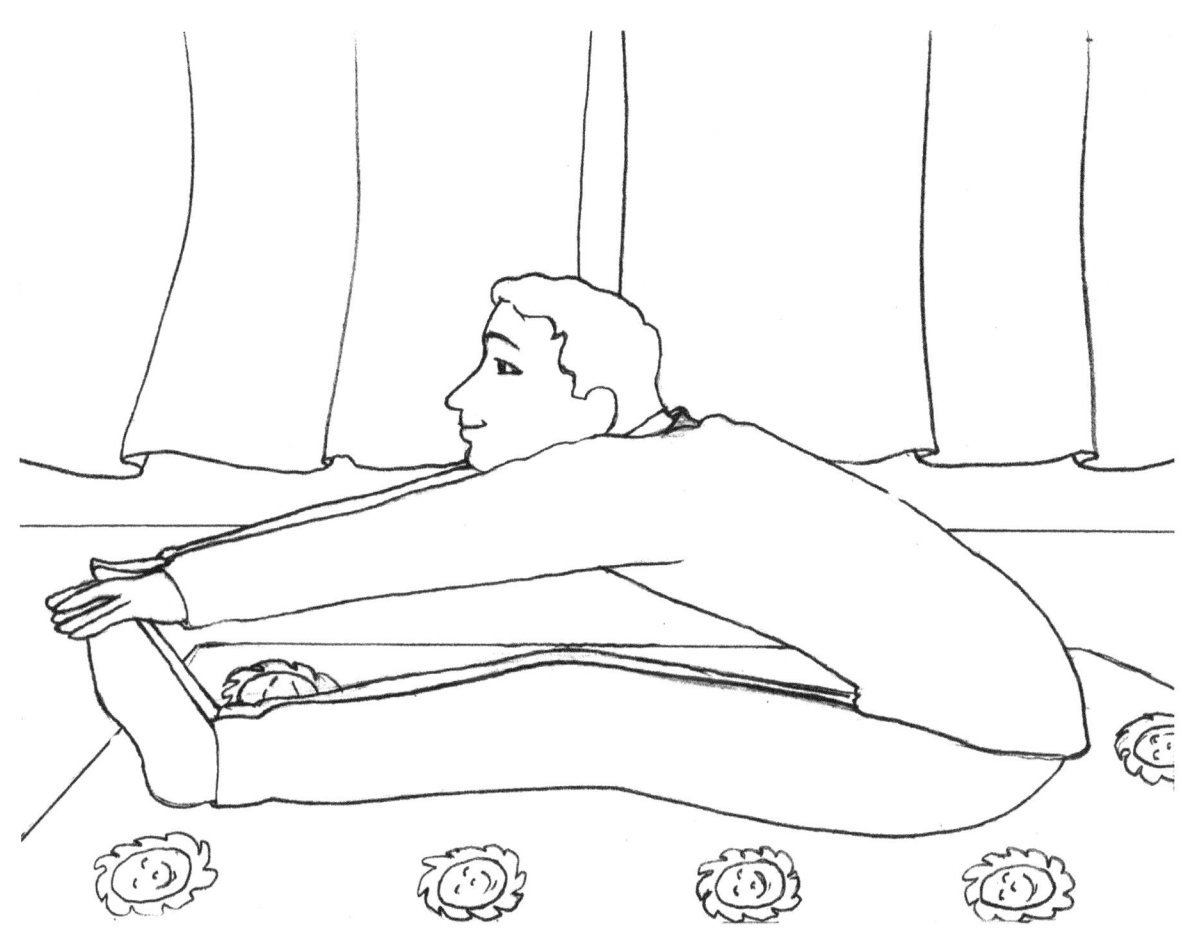

The kids on their mats go round and round,
Round and round, round and round.
The kids on their mats go round and round,
All through yoga class.

# Downward Dog

# Bunny Hop

Put a balloon or ball between your legs and hop like a bunny!

# Donkey Kicks

Keep your head in the air looking forward and kick your feet up in the air one at a time.

# Warrior

The warrior poses build strength in your body.

# Rainbow

Put one hand on the floor with legs stretched out and reach the opposite hand high, stretch out like a rainbow.

# Snake Sliding

Hiss and slither up into snake pose.

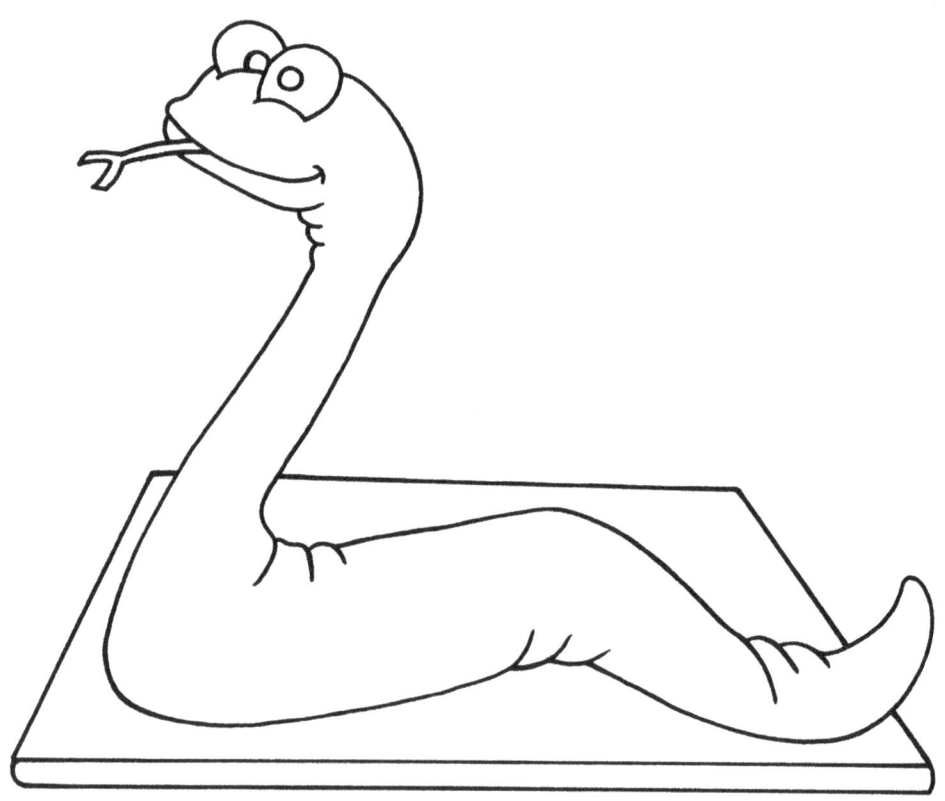

# Metta Meditation

Did you know that Metta is a way to offer love and happiness to ourselves, to people we love, and to all living creatures.

May we be safe
May we be happy
May we be peaceful
May we be healthy
May we walk with love in our hearts

# Balloon Breathing

Raise your arms high, take a deep breath and as you exhale let all the air come out like a balloon.

## What are you grateful for? Write or draw in the space below.

Tell your family and friends how you are feeling.

Draw a face of how you are feeling. Are you happy?
Are you sad? Why?

# Live Yoga

Make healthy choices and actions towards others and yourself. Talk about your feelings and give lots of hugs to those you love.

# Nature

When you are outside notice all the plants and trees around you and be aware as the seasons change.

# Happy Place

What makes you happy? People, animals, places, feelings . . . .
Draw in the space below.

# Operation Smile

Try smiling for one minute.
Did you know smiling is contagious?

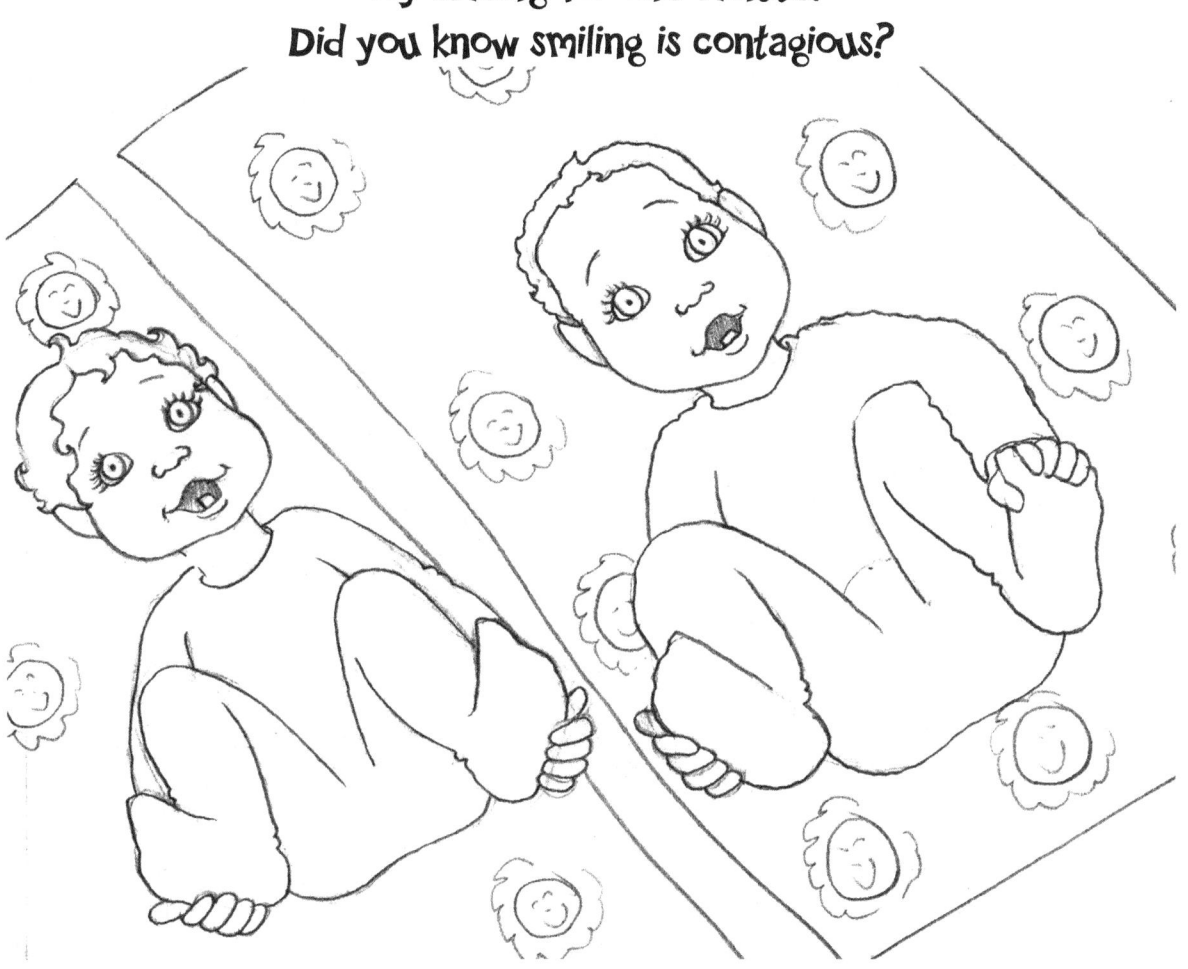

# Today's Day

Remember to treat each day as special just like it was a holiday like Mother's or Father's Day. When someone asks you what day is it, say, "Today's Day."

# Be Kind

Show love to your family and friends, the more you give the more you will receive.

Sing, dance and play instruments to fill yourself with love and happiness.

## Healthy food fuels your body.
## What did you eat that was healthy today?

# Love and Peace

What do you love about your friends and family?
Focus on the things you love!

# Choose Happiness

Write something that makes you happy.

# Appreciation

Start and end your day with identifying one thing you appreciate about the day.

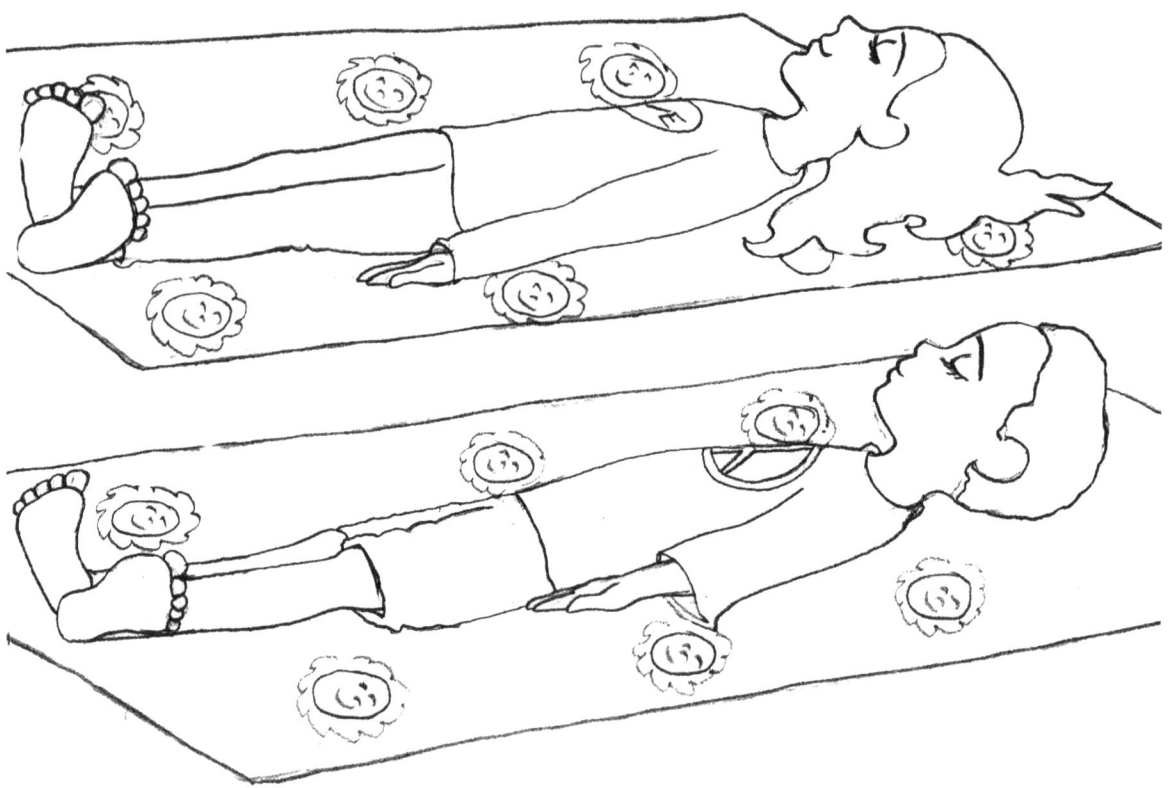

Om is the sound of the universe. Rub your hands, sit up tall, take a deep breathe, Om.

# Playful Namaste

Namaste means I see the light in you and you see the light in me.
Remember to bow to your teacher and your friends after class.
NAMASTE.

Somewhere over the rainbow dreams come true . . . .
always believe in yourself.

# Choose Peace

Draw a peace sign below.

# Books by Kerry

Audrey's Journey - Loving Kindness
Audrey's Journey - Round and Round Yoga
Blaine's Playful Namaste
If It Does Not Grow Say No - Eatable Activities for Kids
Pile of Smile Activity Book

# Notes

# Notes

# Notes

# Notes

# Notes

# Notes

# Notes

# Notes

# Notes

# Notes

www.ingramcontent.com/pod-product-compliance
Lightning Source LLC
Chambersburg PA
CBHW061936290426
44113CB00025B/2933